CW00944411

Dedicated to my mother and my Nana,
who both taught me to use my voice,
gifts, and talents to help make
a difference in the world.

LIFT EVERY VOICE AND CHANGE

A Celebration of Black Leaders and the Words that Inspire Generations

Charnaie Gordon

Illustrated by Aeron Cargill

becker&mayer! kids

YOUR VOICE IS POWERFUL

Have you ever thought about how powerful YOUR own voice can be?

Speaking is the natural way we communicate with one another. Sometimes by speaking we can stand up for things we believe in or stand up for our friends and family members. We can use our voice to state our opinions or express our emotions and feelings. Words can comfort or inspire, and voices can be raised in song or in protest.

Throughout history, Black people have been raising their voices to speak up and speak out. From the Civil Rights movement of the 1960s to the Black Lives Matter movement of today, Black leaders from the past and present day have used their words to help challenge thoughts and ideas or speak out against unfairness and injustices.

Sometimes people think Black history and the Black experience is all about struggle. But Blackness is about so much more than just struggle. It is about light, perseverance, and joy.

The twelve quotes you will read and hear were each spoken by notable Black people from the present day or from the past. These quotes reflect their determination, achievements, wisdom, and the mantras they used or still use to persevere.

You may have learned about some of the people featured in this book at school or saw them on television or on the internet. However, some people may be new to you. There are many Black leaders you may not know who accomplished great achievements not only for themselves but for the Black community. It's important to explore and learn about other pioneers and leaders who may not be celebrated as often as others like Jackie Robinson and Rosa Parks. My hope is that readers will use these quotes to help inspire them, challenge them to do better, or help them see things from a different perspective. Some of the famous quotes in this book gave people from past generations hope and, in some cases, helped change the course of history.

So, use the inspiring words in this book to help challenge your thinking and motivate you to overcome whatever obstacles may come your way. These twelve amazing quotes—from civil rights leader Dr. Martin Luther King Jr.'s call to end segregation, to mathematician Katherine Johnson helping to break gender and race barriers—will help you reflect and find inspiration every month of the year.

What you say matters, so let your voice be heard whenever there is an opportunity to speak. Who knows, by the time you finish this book, you may be inspired to say or write something of your own!

"Cast down your bucket where you are. Cast it down in making friends in every manly way of the people of all races by whom you are surrounded."

Booker T. Washington

Educator, Author

"ATLANTA COMPROMISE"

Speech at the Cotton States and International Exposition

SEPTEMBER 18, 1895

Born enslaved in 1856, Booker T. Washington started working at an early age. He was enthusiastic about hard work and education. He made a tremendous impact on education and his legacy still lives on today.

Booker is best known for his speech The Atlanta Compromise. The agreement said that in exchange for Black Americans having basic rights to education, they would not ask for the right to vote, nor would they fight against racism, segregation, and discrimination. Booker believed that by working hard, Black people would gain the approval of white society, have access to basic education and economic security, and would ensure that the government would respect all their legal rights instead of just some legal rights. And when Booker says "manly" in his speech, he was not giving a standard of how a person should act, but rather everyone as a whole, as humans, in every *hu*-manly way.

Southern whites loved Booker's speech, but highly educated Black people like activist and sociologist W. E. B. Du Bois criticized and rejected it. Du Bois did not agree with tolerating racial segregation or discrimination.

During his lifetime, Booker founded an institution designed to uplift Black Americans. Today that institution is known as Tuskegee University located in Tuskegee, Alabama.

Booker T. Washington and W. E. B. Du Bois had different views on ways to achieve equality. Think about a time when you and a friend had different points of view or opinions about an idea and write about it.

"Even though we face the difficulties of today and tomorrow, I still have a dream."

Dr. Martin Luther King Jr.

Baptist Minister and Social Activist

"I HAVE A DREAM"

Speech at the March on Washington for Jobs and Freedom

AUGUST 28, 1963

Born in 1929, Dr. Martin Luther King Jr. believed in equal rights for all, even as a young boy. During his lifetime, he worked hard to end racial discrimination, segregation, and racism during the Civil Rights movement.

On a red-hot summer day in 1963, Dr. King spoke to a large crowd of people and declared "I have a dream." This speech is one of the most well-known speeches of the last century. It carried a beautiful message of hope for people of all races and ages and helped pave the way for both the Civil Rights Act and the Voting Rights Act to be signed into law by President Lyndon B. Johnson in the 1960s.

Dr. King's poignant words continue to touch hearts and influence the minds of people to pay attention and act. Although there has been some progress since he delivered this monumental speech, there is still so much more to be accomplished to have true equality.

Dr. King dared to dream big even when times were tough. Do you have big dreams for your future? What steps can you take to start putting those dreams into action and be like Dr. King?

"We must urge you to fight now to be the leaders of today, not tomorrow. We've got to be the leaders of today."

During his senior year in high school, Stokely Carmichael became heavily interested in the Civil Rights Movement. In college, he joined groups and organizations like the Student Nonviolent Coordinating Committee (SNCC).

Stokely is known for making the "Black Power" slogan famous. The phrase is a call for Black people to have racial pride, unite in solidarity, and build a sense of community. Stokely helped pave the way for the sit-in movement during the Civil Rights era and the Black Lives Matter movement of today. Stokely started saying that Black lives mattered years ago against the backdrop of the Vietnam War and racism in the late 1960s.

Stokely Carmichael

Civil Rights Activist and Organizer of the Global Pan-African Movement

Black Power Speech

OCTOBER 29, 1966

Even after the "Black Power" movement declined in the late 1970s, its impact continues today. In some ways, the movements of today channel the spirit of Stokely's movement in its efforts to combat racism and the social, economic, and political injustices that continue to affect Black Americans.

Despite others disagreeing with his ideas, Stokely Carmichael continued to speak out against racism and injustice in America. What topics or issues are you willing to stand up for and speak out on even if others do not agree with you?

> ## "A whole new generation of people have assessed and absorbed their history, and, in that tremendous action, have freed themselves of it and will never be victims again."

James Baldwin was a champion for human rights and one of the most prolific authors of the twentieth century. He was born in 1924 in Harlem, New York, during the Harlem Renaissance.

James's passion for writing developed during his teenage years when he wrote his first article in his school's magazine at the age of thirteen. His first novel, entitled *Go Tell It on the Mountain*, was published in 1953.

James was also an important figure of the Civil Rights movement. He wrote about race and the struggles Black Americans faced living in America. His powerful writings and examinations of American culture are still relevant today.

Throughout his life, James was recognized not only for his incredible achievements in literature, but also for his efforts to facilitate understanding and respect between all people. James's influence on the world of books and literature has been very important. Not only does his work inspire others to write, but it also empowers others to read and learn about the Black experience and to fight for their rights.

> James Baldwin once said, "History is not the past. It is the present. We carry our history with us. We are our history." What do you think he meant by this quote?

James Baldwin

Writer and Activist

"An Open Letter to My Sister, Angela Davis"

NOVEMBER 1970

"Language alone protects us from the scariness of things with no names."

Toni Morrison

Novelist, Professor

Nobel Prize in Literature Lecture

DECEMBER 7, 1993

Born in 1931, Toni Morrison's love of literature started as a child. In high school, she began reading the works of Jane Austen and Leo Tolstoy. As an adult, she was the first Black female author to win the Nobel Prize in Literature for her amazing contributions to the arts. Her first novel, *The Bluest Eye*, was published in 1970 and was followed by her second novel, *Sula*, in 1973.

Once called a "national treasure" by President Barack Obama, Toni's writing has inspired generations of readers and writers. Today, her writing still gives people from around the world hope and encouragement. Toni's work forced everyone to pay attention to the words she spoke and wrote while also helping Black people to see themselves reflected on the pages of her books.

Through her writing, Toni made it her goal to encourage the Black community, but especially Black women, to walk in their truth. Her integrity, compassion, and intelligence helped her connect with people of all races and cultures.

Toni Morrison believed in putting Black voices, particularly women's voices, and Black experiences at the center of her work. How can all people ensure that Black voices continue to be heard and amplified in literature?

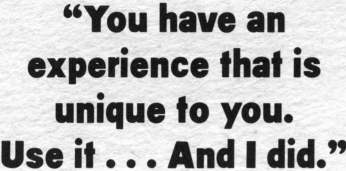

"You have an experience that is unique to you. Use it . . . And I did."

Faith Ringgold

Author, Activist, and Artist Best Known for Her Narrative Quilts

National Visionary Leadership Project Interview on Political Art

MARCH 22, 2010

Faith Ringgold grew up in the 1930s surrounded by influential artists, writers, and activists. She is best known for her children's books and story quilts that communicate her political beliefs. Faith grew up around fabric and got her inspiration for quilting from her mother who was a fashion designer. With her quilts, Faith combines painting, writing, and fabrics to create original and beautiful works of art. Her most famous book, *Tar Beach*, is based on a story quilt from her popular Woman on a Bridge series.

Through her activism, she has opened doors for several Black artists, including herself. She was one of the first women to organize and fight for representation of Black and women artists in museums and galleries.

Faith Ringgold experienced setbacks during her pursuit in becoming an artist. Have you ever experienced a setback and how did you overcome it?

Today, Faith's work remains as important and influential as it was years ago. She continues to influence and inspire people across the world to paint, write, teach, quilt, and create fabric designs.

"When they had briefings, I asked permission to go. And they said, 'Well, the girls don't usually go.' And I said, 'Well, is there a law?'"

Katherine Johnson's love of numbers prepared her for greatness early in life. Born in 1918, Katherine knew women could do the same things as men, so she boldly set out to prove it. During her career, she helped break race and gender barriers in the 1950s when she joined a team of Black women hired by NASA to work as "human computers," meaning they would do all the math and science calculations using their minds only. With her impressive mathematical skills, Katherine helped calculate the flight path for NASA's first space mission in 1962. Her calculations were also important to the success of the Apollo 11 moon landing. Although Katherine's contributions were extremely important to the early success of NASA, it was not until the 2016 release of the movie *Hidden Figures* that she and the other women of NASA received the long overdue recognition they deserved.

Today, Katherine's legacy is still seen and felt. Her achievements continue to inspire new generations of Black girls and women to pursue excellence in mathematics and science and be unafraid to break barriers for women and people of color.

Katherine Johnson questioned the rules by asking if there was a law against allowing women to attend meetings. Why do you think it was so important to her to go to the meetings?

Katherine Johnson

NASA Mathematician, Computer Scientist, "Human Computer"

What Matters
Katherine Johnson: NASA Pioneer and "Computer"

FEBRUARY 25, 2011

"My folks instilled in me such a love for my community, an appreciation of our culture, and such a profound sense of dignity in spite of any trial or tribulation."

Born in 1984 to Nigerian immigrants, Ayọ Tometi is the oldest of three children. Her parents have always been the main source of guidance and encouragement in her life. They taught her the importance of community involvement and service work. At an early age, she began leading both advocacy and council groups.

Ayọ is one of the three co-founders of the Black Lives Matter movement. In 2013, she started the movement with Alicia Garza and Patrisse Cullors. In 2020, Ayọ was named as one of *Time Magazine*'s Most Influential People. Her foundation, Diaspora Rising, is an extension of her commitment to the Black Lives Matter movement.

Ayọ Tometi

Co-Founder of Black Lives Matter, Writer, Human Rights Activist

Marching in the Arc of Justice Conference

MARCH 7, 2015

For the past two decades, Ayọ has been working to create solutions and uplift global Black communities through her important work. She is also fighting racism in technology systems such as facial recognition, a computer system used to recognize people but which often cannot accurately identify features of non-white people.

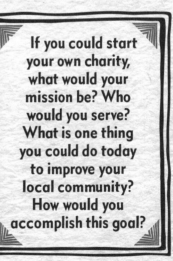

If you could start your own charity, what would your mission be? Who would you serve? What is one thing you could do today to improve your local community? How would you accomplish this goal?

"They set a possibility in motion, passing down through the ages from heart to heart and breath to breath."

Born in 1940, John Lewis set possibility into motion early in life by getting into "good trouble" to help protect human rights. During his teenage years, John, inspired by Dr. Martin Luther King Jr., resolved to join the fight for civil rights. He is best known for being the chairperson of the Student Nonviolent Coordinating Committee (SNCC) and for leading the 1965 march across the Edmund Pettus Bridge in Selma, Alabama protesting racial injustice and violence. John served as a U.S. Representative for the Fifth Congressional District in Georgia from 1987 until his death in 2020. There are currently petitions to rename a voting rights bill and the Edmund Pettus Bridge after the civil rights legend.

John Lewis

Politician and Civil Rights Activist

National Museum of African American History and Culture Opening in Washington, D.C.

SEPTEMBER 24, 2016

How can you be like John Lewis to help inspire your country or community? What sacrifices are you willing to make for others for things you believe in?

A champion of non-violent protests and change, he worked tirelessly and risked his life countless times by challenging racial segregation. John's work has had a tremendous impact on the Black Lives Matter movement. He showed us all what was possible with hard work and dedication, and he also left behind a powerful legacy of social justice for future generations to set into motion.

> **"We have a responsibility to push the conversation forward until we're all equal, 'til we're all equal in this place, because until everyone's free no one's free—and that's just a fact."**

Shawn "Jay-Z" Carter credits his mother with teaching him at an early age to take responsibility for his truth, fight for his freedom, and to live life on his own terms. Not only is Jay-Z called one of the greatest rappers of all time, but he is also a successful business executive, and the first hip-hop artist billionaire. As an entrepreneur, he has his own clothing brand, he is a multi-millionaire investor, and he owns real estate.

For over two decades Jay-Z has continued to climb the ladder of success while also giving back millions to support and empower Black communities. In 2003, Jay-Z started the Shawn Carter Scholarship Foundation with his mom to offer students an opportunity to go to college. As a father and husband, Jay-Z focuses on ensuring his family and children feel loved and supported in a safe environment while also giving them the space and freedom to be who they want to be.

Civil rights activist Fannie Lou Hammer once declared, "Nobody's free until everybody's free," an idea Jay-Z believes in too. Why do you think it is important for present leaders to continue to speak the words of past leaders?

> **"I think we've taken great strides toward equality as far as the positions are concerned. So, if you're a girl, and you're interested in engineering, be an engineer."**

Born in 1931, Gladys Mae West was determined to use education to help her get out of poverty. She worked hard and graduated at the top of her high school class, and she was a first-generation college student in her family.

In 1957, West began her career as a mathematician at the U.S. Naval Base at Dahlgren in Virginia. She was one of a small group of Black women who worked on hand calculations for the military before the invention of computers.

The incredible work Dr. West did during her 42-year career has had a significant and lasting impact on the development of technologies that are currently used in cars, airplanes, and mobile phones. We have her to thank for the technology that led to the Global Positioning System (GPS). Today, billions of people rely on GPS to help them get where they are going by land, air, and sea.

In 2018, Dr. West was inducted into the Air Force Hall of Fame. She continues to speak to elementary students in the Black community and across the world about the importance of studying science, technology, engineering, and mathematics.

> **How do you think the world would be different without GPS? Brainstorm a list of ways you think our lives would be different without this helpful invention.**

> **"You look at these challenges as opportunities, not only for yourself, but when you're first that means you get to open the door. And if you do it right, you get to prop it open."**

Stacey Abrams
Politician, Attorney, Activist, and Author

Sister Circle Live – Stacey Abrams speaks
on a Free & Fair Voting Process

JANUARY 6, 2019

Born in 1973, Stacey Abrams grew up understanding the importance of education and service. As the second oldest of six children, she helped her parents raise her younger siblings.

Stacey also knows a thing or two about being the first person to achieve a major goal. She graduated as the first Black valedictorian of her high school class. In 2018, she was the first Black woman in U.S. history nominated for governor by a major political party.

> **Has there ever been a time when you were the first person to achieve something notable? How were you able to achieve your goal? How did your accomplishment affect you?**

Stacey's passion to provide service and help others inspired her to start Fair Fight, an organization that focuses on promoting free and fair elections and fights against voter suppression, particularly for Black voters. For the 2020 election, she helped register 800,000 new Georgia voters.

Stacey's tenacity and perseverance have helped her go far beyond the ballot box. She continues to use her experience as a politician, author, and lawyer to be a changemaker to help ensure a brighter future for the next generation.

GLOSSARY

ACTIVISM: The action people take when they want to see changes made in their community, school, or in the world.

BLACK LIVES MATTER MOVEMENT: A movement that began in 2013 which calls for people to fight against racism and violence that unfairly affects Black lives.

CIVIL RIGHTS: Civil rights are basic human rights. To have civil rights means each person should be treated the same under the law and have the same basic rights.

CIVIL RIGHTS MOVEMENT: The Civil Rights movement was an ongoing struggle for racial equality between 1954 -1968. Black Americans stood up and protested their right to be treated the same as white people.

THE MARCH ON WASHINGTON: On August 28, 1963, more than 250,000 people gathered and marched in Washington, DC because Black people wanted a fair chance at getting jobs.

CIVIL RIGHTS ACT: The Civil Rights Act of 1964 is one of the most important civil rights laws in the history of the United States. It helped end racial segregation (separating people based on the color of their skin) and protected all people from discrimination.

DISCRIMINATION: Unfair treatment of an individual person or a specific group of people based on the way they act or how they look.

HARLEM RENAISSANCE: A time period during the 1920s when Black American heritage and culture were widely celebrated.in the United States.

RACISM: Treating people unfairly based on their skin color, culture, or heritage.

SEGREGATION: The act of separating specific people or groups of people.

VOTING RIGHTS ACT: A law created in 1965 to help make it easier for Black people to vote in America.

IN YOUR OWN WORDS

Now, it's your turn to write!

Writing can be fun, and it doesn't always involve writing hundreds or thousands of words in a formal structure. Use your imagination and write down your thoughts as they come, in any format you choose. You can write a speech, essay, song, blog post, comic strip, poem, or short story.

In the space below, write or draw whatever you feel inside. Your words are now part of this story, right alongside Dr. King, Stacey Abrams, Jay-Z, and all the other Black voices you've just heard. One day, you too can speak your words in public and change the world!

FURTHER READING

This list of books is for those looking for additional Black history resources. These titles not only give children the resources they need to understand the importance of Black history, but they also shed light on Black voices and perspectives in American history and literature.

To create a more diverse and inclusive library, it is important to empathize with people from different backgrounds. One of the best ways to better understand the experiences of others is through storytelling.

The Juneteenth Story: Celebrating the End of Slavery in the United States by Alliah L. Agostini and Sawyer Cloud

Journey to America: Celebrating Inspiring Immigrants Who Became Brilliant Scientists, Game-Changing Activists & Amazing Entertainers by Maliha Abidi

Young Gifted and Black: Meet 52 Black Heroes from Past and Present by Jamia Wilson and Andrea Pippins

Your Legacy: A Bold Reclaiming of Our Enslaved History by Schele Williams

The People Remember by Ibi Zoboi

Who Are Your People? by Bakari Sellers

Unspeakable: The Tulsa Race Massacre by Carole Boston Weatherford

Opal Lee and What It Means to Be Free: The True Story of the Grandmother of Juneteenth by Alice Faye Duncan

The Year We Learned to Fly by Jacqueline Woodson and Rafael López

The ABCs of Black History by Rio Cortez and Lauren Semmer

ABOUT THE AUTHOR

Charnaie Gordon is a writer, podcast host, and digital creator. She is the author of the picture book *A Kids Book About Diversity* (A Kids Book About, 2021), co-author of *A Friend Like You* (Sleeping Bear Press, 2021) and *A Planet Like Ours* (Sleeping Bear Press, 2022), and editor of *Race Cars: A Children's Book About White Privilege* (Quarto Kids, May 2021). Charnaie serves as a member of the National Advisory Board for Reading is Fundamental for their Race, Equity, and Inclusion (REI) initiative.

Charnaie's blog, Here Wee Read, is where she expresses her creativity and passion for reading, diverse literature, and literacy. In addition to her blog and social media, Charnaie is also the founder of her children's literacy non-profit organization 50 States 50 Books, Inc. (http://50states50books.net) which collects and donates diverse children's books to deserving kids in each of the 50 US states. Find her online at hereweeread.com and @hereweeread on Instagram, Facebook, Twitter, and Pinterest.

ABOUT THE ILLUSTRATOR

Aeron Cargill is a Jamaican American illustrator who has worked on several children's books and textbooks. His art style is a playful blend of whimsical realism with a touch of nostalgia. Aeron loves history and also works as a fine artist and art director. He lives and works in Florida. Visit him at aeroncargill.com.

Brimming with creative inspiration, how-to projects, and useful information to enrich your everyday life, quarto.com is a favorite destination for those pursuing their interests and passions.

© 2023 by Quarto Publishing Group USA Inc.
Illustrations © 2023 by Aeron Cargill

Dr. Martin Luther King Jr. clip reprinted by arrangement with The Heirs to the Estate of Martin Luther King Jr., c/o Writers House as agent for the proprietor New York, NY. Copyright © 1963 by Dr. Martin Luther King, Jr. Renewed © 1991 by Coretta Scott King.

James Baldwin and Stokely Carmichael clips reprinted by arrangement with Pacifica Radio Archives.

Katherine Johnson clip used courtesy WHRO Public Media.

Faith Ringgold clip used with special thanks to The National Visionary Leadership Project (NVLP).

All sound clips are public domain unless otherwise noted.

First published in 2023 by becker&mayer Kids!, an imprint of The Quarto Group,
142 West 36th Street, 4th Floor, New York, NY 10018, USA
T (212) 779-4972 F (212) 779-6058 www.Quarto.com

All rights reserved. No part of this book may be reproduced in any form without written permission of the copyright owners. All images in this book have been reproduced with the knowledge and prior consent of the artists concerned, and no responsibility is accepted by producer, publisher, or printer for any infringement of copyright or otherwise, arising from the contents of this publication. Every effort has been made to ensure that credits accurately comply with information supplied. We apologize for any inaccuracies that may have occurred and will resolve inaccurate or missing information in a subsequent reprinting of the book.

becker&mayer Kids! titles are also available at discount for retail, wholesale, promotional, and bulk purchase. For details, contact the Special Sales Manager by email at specialsales@quarto.com or by mail at The Quarto Group, Attn: Special Sales Manager, 100 Cummings Center Suite 265D, Beverly, MA 01915 USA.

10 9 8 7 6 5 4 3 2 1

ISBN: 978-0-7603-7459-7

Publisher: Rage Kindelsperger
Creative Director: Laura Drew
Art Director: Scott Richardson
Managing Editor: Cara Donaldson
Text: Charnaie Gordon
Design: Scott Richardson

MIX
Paper | Supporting responsible forestry
FSC® C122384

Printed in China

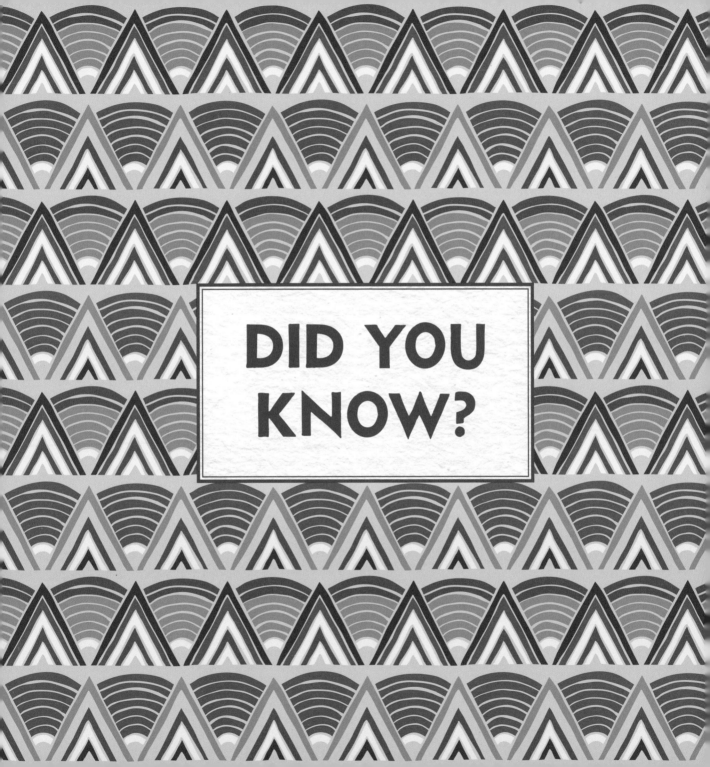

DID YOU KNOW?